LIVING IN COLOR

COLOR IN CONTEMPORARY INTERIOR DESIGN

4

COLORING A ROOM OF ONE'S OWN
STELLA PAUL

11

A LIFE LIVED IN COLOR
INDIA MAHDAVI

14

LIVING IN COLOR

218

DIRECTORIES

226

INDEX

COLORING A ROOM OF ONE'S OWN
STELLA PAUL

"COLOR IS A VITAL NECESSITY. IT IS A RAW MATERIAL,
INDISPENSABLE TO LIFE, LIKE WATER AND FIRE." [1]
FERNAND LÉGER (1881-1955)

The colors of the rooms we inhabit reflect us. They tell stories about identity, taste, and culture. Color permeates everything. Color provides more than a backdrop for living out our lives. It's central, ubiquitous in our surroundings as well as in our thoughts and dreams, equally driving everything from utilitarian functions, to emotional state, to spiritual expression. We perceive color through complex processes of physiological input and mental analysis. Great thinkers have devoted countless efforts to understanding its workings, yet we are constantly dazzled by new insights even as we are confounded by unsolvable mysteries. We attempt to harness color by constructing elaborate competing systems for its organization. We try to define the ineffable and translate the visual into language—ricocheting from evocative, near-poetical terms to dryly numerical symbols for communicating what we see. Even so, we don't see eye-to-eye. We can't be sure that what one person sees (let alone what one feels) is the same as another's perception. Nevertheless, we find immense pleasure in cocooning ourselves with luscious color and affirming its powerful allures—whether we seek in it vibrantly unbridled revelry, or measured intellectual restraint, or soothing evocations of tranquility. It has always been that way. No matter how far back in history, people ask color to work its magic in spaces that mean the most to them. Color speaks to us. What, then, on its most fundamental level, is color?

"COLORS ARE THE DEEDS AND SUFFERING OF LIGHT." [2]
JOHANN WOLFGANG VAN GOETHE (1749-1832)

Color is light. But we didn't always know that. It was revolutionary when Isaac Newton teased apart the spectrum's constituent wavelengths in 1666. When sunlight ("white light") passed through Newton's prism, the sunbeam bent at varying angles to reveal colors as separate rays, each with its own precise wavelength. Newton then clinched his argument by passing the colored rays through a second prism, recombining all the colors into reconstituted white light.

When light hits a surface, some wavelengths are absorbed while others are bounced back; the waves that are reflected back signal its color. To see color in its manifestation as light, it takes a complex interplay between the physics of light's behaviors, the physiology and mechanics of an individual's eyes, and the unique analysis by each person's brain.

We're not alone in seeing color. But other animals see things very differently, with vision apparatus unlike ours. Dogs see the world only through wavelengths that translate to yellow and blue. There's no red or green in their worldview. Some butterflies see worlds of color unattainable by us, having more elaborate color receptors than humans. We can distinguish about ten million colors. But the field of electromagnetic energy available to human vision is just a small swath of a much larger bandwidth. Energy transmitted as wavelengths that we can't see with our eyes extends through infrared and ultraviolet light. And some species not only see these realms invisible to us, but those "invisible" colors play enormous roles in survival and propagation. Snakes have access to infrared, seeing heat from warm-blooded prey. Birds and bees see ultraviolet markings on plants and flowers that depend on pollination: patterning invisible to us. The living world is color coded. Colors we see as well as those we can't perceive show what is delectable or poisonous, what or whom to avoid or approach, whether to be afraid or aroused. Survival depends on color. Some animals change their colors to match their circumstances. In under a second, octopi (although color-blind) transform their skin into colors mimicking their surroundings. Human beings can't do the same, but we can reflect our moods in our environments—through color we surround ourselves with.

"COLOR DECEIVES CONTINUALLY." [3]
JOSEF ALBERS (1888-1976)

After revealing light's color waves, Newton took the further step of schematizing his rainbow of colors—the spectrum—into an arrangement of seven discreet hues in specific order. More than 350 years later we still use his scheme: red, orange, yellow, green, blue, indigo, and violet. It's purely an abstraction. The electromagnetic field is continuous; boundaries are subtle and fluid. Why break the field into exactly seven hues? Why include two colors, blue and indigo, that are so similar? Newton imposed order. Among other ideals, his concept of color regulation mirrored organizing rules for musical octaves. Any form of color organization is an imposition of some form of ideal order. Newton wasn't the first. In antiquity, Aristotle had a color scale, too, to show his belief that colors were formed through mixtures of darkness and lightness. So white was at one end and its polar opposite, black, at the other. Blue lies close to black because it's seen as an extreme of darkness. Aristotle's concept endured even through Renaissance Europe, thousands of years later.

Philosophers, scientists, artists, designers, and poets in every century theorized about how to organize color into coherent systems—and how to create harmony. And with every inquiry, what looked unequivocal in one framework could easily be disputed in another. Johann Wolfgang von Goethe didn't accept Newton's seemingly objective physics. He published his own color theories, which he considered his most important work. Goethe insisted on subjectivity, organizing colors into "plus" and "minus" categories according to specific sensations. Every hue is a trigger, leading alternately to melancholia or serenity. Some colors excite quick, lively feelings; others make a restless, anxious impression; others are powerful, radiant, or "splendid." The idea that even before it's an aesthetic issue, color performance is a psychological one tantalized people long before Goethe and continues long after.

> "FULL SATURATED COLORS HAVE AN EMOTIONAL SIGNIFICANCE I WANT TO AVOID." [4]
> LUCIAN FREUD (1922-2011)

Color begins in the physical but ends up in the psyche. Can anyone rightly predict responses to color? Although people in every period try, eagerly wanting to universalize, color is impossible to pin down. Reactions to color are tinted by our associations from childhood and our habits, shared cultural preconditioning, and personal idiosyncrasies. Carl Jung saw color as a symbolic language that might be decoded like a cipher: red stands for blood, blue for the spiritual. But someone else could find red implies romance or privilege, or insist that blue means loyalty or melancholy. Green could suggest envy, but also nature. Piet Mondrian linked the color so strongly to landscapes (anathema for him when he was creating purely abstract art) that he went to great length to avoid even looking out windows that opened onto fields and trees. He didn't want to color his thoughts. For a while, Richard Diebenkorn eliminated blue from his palette for the same reasons—too redolent of landscape when trying to think about abstraction.

Many psychologists in addition to Jung have read into color keys to the unconscious, seeking ways to measure or define impacts. Max Lüscher's mid-century color test revealed basic personality traits through subjects' ranked color preferences to 73 color swatches. A strong preference to blue shows a need for peace and tranquility. A predisposition to black and red mean suppressed excitement, which threatens to discharge itself in aggressive impulses and emotional violence. It's the ultimate red flag: "what cannot be mastered will be destroyed." A lot of color psychology reveals more about the interpreter and his or her cultural milieu than about people in general, or even individual subjects. But the work goes on.

Studies to measure colors' powers to control behavior are often linked to workplace productivity or sales and marketing. Rooms with colored lighting or walls are assessed on the subjects' sense of elapsed time: supposedly overestimated in red environments. Red has also been judged to make things seem bigger and affect pulse and blood pressure. When quickening the pace is desirable, such as in a fast-food restaurant, red is supposed to attract, stimulate excitement and move consumers along. Buyer beware, though. Studies are as fluid and inexact as is the concept of decoding specific emotions engendered by color. Market research by color associations and producers of consumer goods make much of color forecasting, with competing annual predictions billed as newsworthy announcements—and cause for us to surround ourselves with new products to embody the present moment.

Color and well-being have been linked forever. One contemporary study of blue light claims it decreases suicidal impulses, and even prompted the installation of blue lighting in selected train stations in Japan. But color's curative powers are as elusive (and longstanding) as color's poetic powers. In antiquity, colored gemstones were thought to contain colored light, used to both diagnose and cure disease. Chromotherapy was in vogue thousands of years later, in the belief that colored light would alter bodily function. Actually, we still use blue light as therapy to break down bilirubin in jaundiced infants, but we can't claim in it any broader or more nebulous overall well-being.

"COLOR! WHAT A DEEP AND MYSTERIOUS LANGUAGE,
THE LANGUAGE OF DREAMS." [5]
PAUL GAUGUIN (1848-1903)

No language is precise or poetically nuanced enough to adequately describe color. Our eyes can discern millions of colors, yet the average English-speaking nonspecialist might use about a dozen terms for talking about color. We hardly have the words to summon basic hue, let alone what happens to color when textured or coated surfaces make light (and color) change dramatically. What do we even mean by hue? If fifty people were to conjure up "red," Josef Albers famously said, there would be fifty different kinds of red in their minds' eyes, with no two alike. Fire-engine red, crimson, merlot, brick red, vermilion, oxblood—all red—look wildly different. We accept remarkably broad categories to bind together things that are diverse, rarely elaborating. From stridently saturated cobalt blue to the most brooding, deepest midnight blue to a wan, powdery sky blue: all are blue. Velvety matte black is totally different from crystalline, glossy black. Should we use the same word for them?

Whether we have many words or few to draw upon, the fact is that humans go to great trouble to create a name for something. And cultures label colors differently. The English word "blue" encompasses an ocean of different tints and shades, but they seem (to us) to share a kinship. In Russian, there are two distinct words for what we categorize as one. Lighter and darker blue are classified separately. In Navajo, one word encompasses all of green and blue together, but uses two separate words for different types of black. It seems that not every language even has words for color names; the Pirahã, a remote Amazonian tribe, have none in their lexicon. Assigning words to sensory experience is a translation, and the disparate ways cultures group and categorize colors speaks to different ways of looking at the world.

Sometimes we impose abstractions of language on visual experiences, and these labels eventually become accepted as fact-based givens rather than idea-based analogies. Do colors really divide into "warm" and "cool"? Red and orange are tacitly warm, and blue epitomizes cool. In reality this is flipped. A heated object starts out red-hot but will glow white-hot with higher temperatures, eventually reaching blue-hot. But color language is not literal; it's analogue. And it can't be denied that deep blue waters suggest refreshing coolness. In other words, whatever label we impose might be concurrently apt or not. Color is impossible to pin down.

Much effort has gone into attempts to communicate clearly what is meant when discussing colors, or matching them across media for commercial production. Color systems have proliferated for centuries, articulating relationships between colors by charting color ranges in diagrams that take the shape of scales, circles or wheels, triangles, or stars. Globes and more complicated three-dimensional models attempt to go a step further, even, in communicating about color, making clear that hue alone does not describe color. Colors have three attributes, and although they work together, each can be teased out as a separate characteristic: hue, value, and saturation. One of many systems, A. H. Munsell's 1905 "Color Notation" shows every hue's gradations in value (or brightness) as well as saturation (or purity) of color. Using complex mathematical formulae to organize the individual colors in their sequences, Munsell's ideal was to define standards that could be readily grasped across platforms. These systems weren't purely theoretical; Munsell stressed the need for a system in order to "avoid mistakes and disappointments" that were inevitable with the available fuzzy descriptors. He wasn't the only one. The Pantone color system, a large, fanning deck of precisely scaled color swatches, originally serviced the printing industry but soon took a broader mandate to encompass color description in all arenas. There have been many national color boards across the world, international bodies such as the C.I.E. (Commission International de l'Éclairage), and standard units in many commercial enterprises such as wall paint companies. Colorimeters and spectrophotometers can now measure and identify color characteristics to an unprecedented degree, in principle making it possible to unequivocally describe color.

But with all those tools at hand, we still turn to poetic language to label the colors we're drawn to. The birth of Marie Antoinette's son set off a decorating craze for a color called "Caca Dauphin," a hue redolent of the infant prince's soiled diapers. Today, paint companies lure twenty-first-century tastes with wall paints called "Life Lesson," "Dead Salmon," "Salty Tear," "Three Legs," and "Thread Needle," or some of many variants on breath, including "Elephant's Breath," "Mole's Breath," or "Wind's Breath." The words vaguely conjure mood (if not hue). Alternately, some names for paint colors strike references that are anything but vague: "Nacho Cheese," "Mayonnaise," "Cheese Powder," or "Bagel." Whether one wants to live in an ethereal world of breathy whisper or one that brazenly celebrates the most ordinary foodstuffs without sugar-coating their quotidian origins, we can find the products to shape our own ambience with color.

"EVERY ROOM HAS ITS GLOOM, THE GREAT THING
IS TO FIND THE COLOR THAT WILL CUT THE GLOOM." [6]
GERTRUDE STEIN (1874-1946)

Color has always been central in designing spaces that are important to us. It can signal rank, ritual, and belief in addition to personal and cultural tastes and states of mind. All are embedded in the nuances of color just as clearly as they are communicated through scale (be it intimate or monumental), or proportion, or the vocabulary of formal and decorative elements.

An urge to paint walls is at our foundation of being. We don't know who they were, what they did inside the interior spaces they created, or why they colored caves' walls with browns, russets, blacks, and whites, but paleolithic individuals at the most liminal stage of our prehistory were already using color masterfully to articulate interior spaces. Earth's silica, clay, and iron oxides were coaxed from friable ocher rocks to create worlds of enchantment: anatomically detailed renderings of animals as well as human handprints. Although we can't understand these earliest records of spectacularly colored interior spaces, we can be awed by their beauty and their mysterious power as well as the technical skill these cave walls reveal.

    Rendering colorful scenes of ritual or symbolic meaning—transforming interior walls into magical environments that tell mythic narrative stories or depict dreamy illusionistic landscapes—has been inextricable to shaping significant interior spaces in many periods throughout our history, and in many cultures. Wall treatment by ancient Egyptians, or Mayans, or Babylonians is richly colored. Walls of Roman antiquity or Renaissance Europe attest to color, too. Frescos, not flat wall color, made walls into vivid protagonists instead of an unobtrusive sideline. Excavations at Pompei in 1748 captivated people everywhere, revealing brilliant rooms frozen in time by Vesuvius's cataclysmic eruption in 79 CE. Not for the first time—and not for the last—contemporary attitudes about living with color took inspiration from rooms of the past. A taste for Pompeian red still reverberates. In truth, many of the historical spaces that spark tastes centuries (or millennia) later are altered by time. Rooms of the past are not always perfect time capsules of their periods. For example, Greek architecture was vividly colored, not white. Thousands of years wore away the colored surfaces. But that didn't stop centuries of taste-makers from embracing the purity of stark white, and creating new white spaces under the influence of an expression they considered ideal—even though historically inaccurate. Le Corbusier saw the gleaming white Parthenon and celebrated its transformation into something white, not colored: "Thank God, time got the better of it and I salute the reconquered monochrome." To strip away color has often stood for stripping away frivolity and excess—sometimes signaling moral and spiritual ideals. Such is the case with Protestant Reformation church interiors, where sober, unembellished white was embraced as the perfect expression of abstemious spirit. Colors (including white and black) are beacons of underlying thought. Just enter a medieval cathedral to be transported by stained-glass windows that narrate significance through colored light. Or consider the use of glazed tiles in the soaring interior of many mosques, where light and color embody ideals of harmony, reverence, and transcendence.

    Where some cultural moments seem to call for stripping away color, others welcome it—sometimes even for the florid excess that it might represent. Walls in luxurious villas at Pompei are not only brilliant. They are lavish. Color can be expensive, especially Pompei's red walls made from cinnabar, a substance that came from far away, was difficult to mine and work with, and cost dearly. Red rooms seemed to be everywhere in newly excavated Pompei, but some of them were actually yellow in their time. Volcanic gases chemically changed pigments. Some of those rooms had also used less expensive shortcuts to making a red environment, by painting a thin red wash on top of a yellow surface. Other rooms are unmitigated cinnabar, and their color saliently reflects their inhabitant's wealth as well as taste.

Red is not alone as a mark of prestige. Purple has long histories across several media as a coveted substance that's hard to get, expensive, and even restricted by law in some periods. To be "born in the purple" isn't merely idiomatic. The offspring of reigning Byzantine rulers were literally born in a room clad with porphyry, a rare purple stone. Sourcing materials for colors' almost always tells an important story, whether it's about the cost of taste or breakthroughs in technologies that introduce new access to color of all kinds. Available materials (and colors) change in every period. The burgeoning new chemistry of synthetic color formulae in the nineteenth century changed public taste in every medium. Brighter greens, chrome yellows, and artificial ultramarine and other blues were newly available and affordable. The color of rooms changed accordingly. New synthetic binders and resins for paints and other products that fill our homes constantly push our tastes in new directions and offer new options for exploiting color behaviors. Textures and light-play metamorphose colors and ask us to equally consider color's core attributes of value and intensity in addition to its family of hue.

Our world is color coded both by nature and by human design. Color fulfills desires, telegraphs attitudes and tastes, and even controls behaviors. Is it any wonder that we ask color to play the lead in the spaces we care about deeply?

1. Fernand Léger, "Color is a vital necessity" from "Color in the World," *Functions of Painting*, 1938, translated edition of 1973, New York: Viking, p. 119.
2. Johann Wolfgang von Goethe, "Colors are the deeds" quoted in Arthur Zajonc, *Catching the Light: The Entwined History of Light and the Mind*, New York and Oxford: Oxford University Press, 1993, p. 210.
3. Joseph Albers, "Interaction of Color", 1963, Yale University Press, New Haven and London, p. 1.
4. Lucian Freud, "Full saturated colors have an emotional significance" quoted in exh.cat *Lucian Freud: Naked portraits, Werke der 40er bis 90er Jahre (Works from the 1940s to the 1990s)*, ed. Jean-Christophe Ammann et al, Frankfurt am Main, 2001.
5. Paul Gauguin, *The Writings of a Savage*, ed by Daniel Guerin, New York. quoted in the 1996 edition.
6. Gertrude Stein, "Every room has its gloom" from Gertrude Stein, *Everybody's Autobiography*, 1937, from New York: Random House 1973 vintage edition reprint.

A LIFE LIVED IN COLOR
INDIA MAHDAVI

I often define myself as a polyglot and polychrome, because I associate colors and cultures with ease. Colors have become my mode of expression precisely because they embody the artistic freedom that I seek. They are the light and shadow of all the souths from which I originate, and they relate the nostalgia of a paradise lost that sparks within me the desire to imagine others. Colors are like the consequences of my memories, of a woven heritage: my mother's Egypt, my father's Iran, our travels while I was still a child, the France we settled in, my own roaming as an architect and designer.

I believe that colors constitute our shared heritage, a common bond between all humans, a mark of our *Homo sapien* identity. Colors play an essential role in nature because they provide beauty, and, for me, beauty lies at the heart of our history: it is the driving force of evolution. I think that we underestimate the importance of color in our lives. It's not only about intelligence, strength, or size. I sometimes think that Darwin underestimated the role that beauty plays in the survival of species, in all species, humans, of course, but also animals and plants.

Color is also a mark of identification to recognize oneself, or to mark a sense of belonging to a group, a tribe, or a family. I became aware of this during my latest trip to Iran, when I visited one of its main carpet workshops. Color plays a crucial role: it allows each tribe to distinguish itself from others by assigning a specific color to their carpets, in the same way that Scottish clans have a distinct tartan pattern.

In my work, in all of my creations, I seek to find the colors of my childhood. It is this rediscovered nostalgia that moves me, that inspires me. I grew up in the United States as a child. I remember watching the Technicolor Tex Avery cartoons on television and their dazzling colors that sparkled in my eyes. It left a permanent mark on me—just like cinema did. The small and big screens are to me, an infinite source of color—and thus inspiration.

The use of color is natural to me, it has never been artificial. It's instinctive and felt—more than it is conscious. When I see a space for the first time, color emerges. It emerges like a feeling. I feel colors. I think my psyche, just as my body, are synesthetic: each color is related to an emotion, to a smell, to a gesture, to a vision, to an impression . . . It has become my expression.

I strive to create ephemeral memories of places, a memory that leaves a mark on the person who visits and discovers the spaces I create. When I design a space—whether it is a restaurant, a hotel, or a private residence that must become the owner's portrait—I seek to bring out a strong and accentuated identity. And the most direct and spontaneous way to achieve this is through color.

Certain colors belong to certain places. For the hotel Condesa in Mexico City, I instinctively chose turquoise. It was the neighborhood's most popular color. It was its very own identity. I simply could not have chosen another color than this very particular shade of blue, to which I gave another identity by using it in a very different context. When I choose a color, it's often for unobvious reasons. Colors bear ancient significations that are concealed and classical. I strive to give them a new meaning beyond their commonly accepted definition. I try to push them beyond their limits, beyond their boundaries while questioning tradition.

Colors help me to take possession of a place—to provoke its true nature. Hence I seek the "right color"—a perfect dialogue between a space and its color. It's a way of celebrating and revealing a space's true depth. For example, when Mourad Mazouz approached me to take over the design of his London restaurant Sketch, I was immediately surprised by the place's eclectic intensity. I felt overwhelmed. And then, the idea of pink came to mind. Pink as a dominant color that helped to restore the space's balance and bring freshness and lightness, a childish frivolity pushed to an extreme. This choice was meant to be temporary, as Mourad wanted to change the decor every two years. However, the Gallery at Sketch and its radical pink were so successful that this unexpected color became its hallmark and deep-rooted identity.

For more than twenty years, I've imagined places, spaces, objects, and stories with the help of color. They have naturally become my friends, my allies. I invite them in to every space and in every object. They follow me everywhere I go. The more, the merrier. Our infinite conversation isn't mundane nor is it nagging—I like them to fight, argue, have a conversation, then comfort each other, reconcile, and love each other again. Colors live in me—and with me. Colors are like words. Each association generates a different meaning, like in a sentence. Such-and-such association reinforces or tames their intensity. I often speak of my colors as an alphabet, a grammar. They are my secondary mother tongue.

To give a new meaning to colors, I carry two secret weapons at all times. My very own palette of paint, that I specifically created with Mériguet-Carrère—it has fifty-two cards, like a deck of playing cards. I also have a velvet palette, crafted by Pierre Frey, the great textile artisan. I named it "True Velvet," with David Lynch's movie in mind. Every card is composed of three velvets—including one that clashes with the other two, that interferes with it. This unusual discrepancy is very practical: it keeps my eye on guard, it helps me find alliances that seem impossible but that secretly provoke beauty.

In my line of work, I seek to celebrate joy, I want the places that I invent to carry energy. Color has the power to fight sadness. It isn't a coincidence if children and elderly people are attracted to color and energies. Children look around, they are born with their eyes wide open, seized by the power of color. Elderly people, those who have seen it all, only seek the most important, the strongest colors. In the end, all that is left is color. It kindles the burst of life that seizes the eye. My intimate relationship with color has allowed the public to recognize my spaces and my creations. Better still, color has allowed me to differentiate myself. To find a place that is mine.

> They are my virtues, my sisters.
> They're a part of my every day, of my creations.
> They're dear to me, my colors.

LIVING IN COLOR

Living Room, New York City Apartment — New York, New York, USA — 2010
Barbara Dente (interior design); Jean Nouvel (architecture)

Dining Area, Art Dealer's Loft — Long Island City, New York, USA — 2008
Steve Blatz

Living and Dining Area, Art Dealer's Loft — Long Island City, New York, USA — 2008
Steve Blatz

Entrance, Lakeside House — Wayzata, Minnesota, USA — 2013
Michelle Andrews

Bathroom, Brighton Residence — Brighton, Victoria, Australia — 2020
Golden

Bathroom, Lafayette Street Residence — New York, New York, USA — 2004
Solveig Fernlund and Neil Logan

Bedroom, Von Teese Residence — Los Angeles, California, USA — 2018
Dita Von Teese

Bedroom, Townhouse — New York, New York, USA — 2014
Studio Piet Boon

Bedroom, Studio — Brooklyn, New York, USA — 2010
Snarkitecture

Entrance, Private Residence — Frankfurt, Germany — 2016
Joseph Dirand

Sitting Room, North Hill Residence — London, England, UK — 2018
Faye Toogood

Living Room, Greenwich Village Residence — New York, New York, USA — 2013
Rafael de Cárdenas

Bedroom, Park Avenue Apartment — New York, New York, USA — 2018
Thomas Pheasant Studio

Bedroom, Manhattan Apartment — New York, New York, USA — 2011
Jenny Dyer

Living Room, Belnord Apartment — New York, New York, USA — 2018
Rafael de Cárdenas

Dining Area, Penthouse Bunker — Berlin, Germany — 2008
Christian Boros

Living Room, Xanadune Residence — Southampton, New York, USA — 2019
Wesley Moon

Reading Nook, Vester Voldgade Residence — Copenhagen, Denmark — 2020
Studio David Thulstrup

Living Room, Palau de Casavelis, Galeria Miquel Azueta — El Baix Empordà, Girona, Spain — 2019
Studioilse

Bedroom, Hidden Ridge Residence — Hidden Hills, California, USA — 2018
Martyn Lawrence Bullard

Living Room, Bel Air Residence — Los Angeles, California, USA — 2018
Sara Story Design

Living Room, Miami Beach Oceanfront Residence — Miami, Florida, USA — 2018
SheltonMindel

Living Room, Park Avenue Apartment — New York, New York, USA — 2018
Thomas Pheasant Studio

Drawing Room, New York City Townhouse — New York, New York, USA — 2013
Ann Pyne, McMillen

Family Room, Buckhead Residence — Atlanta, Georgia, USA — 2018
Suzanne Kasler Interiors

Living and Dining Room, Georgetown Cottage — Washington, D.C., USA — 2016
Mary Douglas Drysdale

Living Room, Southampton Cottage — Southampton, New York, USA — 2012
Ann Pyne, McMillen

Salon, Pedro Espírito Santo Residence — Lisbon, Portugal — 2015
Pedro Espírito Santo

Bedroom, Malibu Residence — Malibu, California, USA — 2012
Kelly Wearstler

Bedroom, Château Fourcas-Hosten — Bordeaux, France — 2013
Michael Coorengel and Jean-Pierre Calvagrac

Bedroom, New Jersey Country Home — New Jersey, USA — 2012
Cullman & Kravis

Bedroom, Betsey Johnson Residence — Malibu, California, USA — 2016
Betsey Johnson

Entrance, Houston Residence — Houston, Texas, USA — 2013
Redd Kaihoi

Yellow Room, The Farm — Sharon, Connecticut, USA — 2019
Michael Trapp

Bedroom, Cap Cana Residence — Cap Cana, Dominican Republic — 2011
Juan Montoya Design

Living Room, London House — London, England, UK — 1987
Anthony Collett

Dressing Room, Bellagio Residence — Los Angeles, California, USA — 2011
Kelly Wearstler

Bedroom, MJ Residence — Undisclosed Location — 2010
Studio Daminato

Living Room, Hotel Particulier Apartment — Paris, France — 2015
Roberto Peregalli and Laura Sartori Rimini, Studio Peregalli

Living Room, Malibu Residence — Malibu, California, USA — 2012
Kelly Wearstler

Living and Dining Room, Pool House, Villa Peduzzi — Lake Como, Lombardy, Italy — 2019
Studio Daminato

Living Room, Lechner House — Los Angeles, California, USA — 2016
Pamela Shamshiri

Studio, The Old Red Schoolhouse — Middletown, Rhode Island, USA — 2014
John Peixinho

Living Room, Sky High Residence — Yellowstone, Montana, USA — 2016
Ken Fulk

Guest Room, Provincetown Residence — Provincetown, Massachusetts, USA — 2014
Ken Fulk

Living Room, Casa Foa — Santiago, Chile — 2017
Grisanti & Cussen

Bedroom, Ski Retreat — Rocky Mountains, USA — 2015
Peter Marino

Drawing Room, Parisian Pied-à-terre — Paris, France — 2006
Alidad

Dressing Room, Madison Avenue Residence — New York, New York, USA — 2017
Kelly Wearstler

Living Room, Pebble Beach Residence — Monterrey, California, USA — 2013
J. P. Molyneux Studio

Dining Room, Manhattan Townhouse — New York, New York, USA — 2014
Laura Santos Interiors

Estlin's Room, Irving Place Carriage House — Brooklyn, New York, USA — 2015
LOT-EK

Home Office, Fifth Avenue Apartment — New York, New York, USA — 2011
Robert Couturier

Bedroom, Elias Residence — São Paulo, Brazil — 2000
Jorge Elias

Den, Molster Residence — Richmond, Virginia, USA — 2018
Janie Molster

Bedroom, Brooklyn Heights Townhouse — Brooklyn, New York, USA — 2010
Kathryn Scott Design Studio

Kitchen, Château de Montigny — Normandy, France — 1999
Andrew Allfree

Master Bedroom, Trey Trust Residence — Los Angeles, California, USA — 2007
Stephen Samuelson, Plan A Architecture

Dining Room, Private Residence — New York, New York, USA — 2012
Jay Jeffers

Entrance, Franklin Hills Residence — Los Angeles, California, USA — 2019
Reath Design

Home Office, Spanish Colonial Revival House — Los Angeles, California, USA — 2015
Thomas Callaway

Library, New York City Townhouse — New York, New York, USA — 2013
Ann Pyne, McMillen

Home Office, Revivalist Mansion — Chicago, Illinois, USA — 2019
Steven Gambrel, S.R. Gambrel (interior design); Liederbach & Graham (architecture)

Living Room, Sarise and Stephen Dweck Residence — Jersey Shore, New Jersey, USA — 2008
Stephen Dweck

Library, Palmolive Apartment — Chicago, Illinois, USA — 2015
Steven Gambrel, S.R. Gambrel (interior design); Liederbach & Graham (architecture)

Living Room, Pied-à-terre — San Francisco, California, USA — 2014
Thomas Britt

Library, Pied-à-terre — San Francisco, California, USA — 2014
Thomas Britt

Living Room, Achille Salvagni Atelier — London, England, UK — 2017
Achille Salvagni

Entry, Darlinghurst Apartment — Sydney, New South Wales, Australia — 2019
Greg Natale

Dining Room, Darlinghurst Apartment — Sydney, New South Wales, Australia — 2019
Greg Natale

The Library, Park Avenue Apartment — New York, New York, USA — 2019
Cindy Adams

Media Room, St. Kilda Residence — Melbourne, Victoria, Australia — 2019
Doherty Design Studio

Meditation Loft, Trey Trust Residence — Los Angeles, California, USA — 2007
Stephen Samuelson, Plan A Architecture

Living Room, Asolo Residence — Asolo, Italy — 2018
Michela Goldschmied

Living Room, Jaipur Jewel Apartment — Rajasthan, India — 2010
Liza Bruce and Nicholas Alvis Vega

Child's Bedroom, Richard and Lisa Perry Penthouse — New York, New York, USA — 2007
Anthony Ingrao

Living Room, Chelsea Loft, Rashid Residence — New York, New York, USA — 2003
Karim Rashid

Living Room, Minimal Fantasy Apartment — Madrid, Spain — 2020
Patricia Bustos Studio

Bedroom, Wine Beach Residence — Rockaway Park, New York, USA — 2011
BNO Design

Breakfast Room, Palm Beach Residence — Palm Beach, Florida, USA — 2016
Bunny Williams

Bedroom, Williams Residence — Beverly Hills, California, USA — 2018
Kravitz Design in collaboration with Disco Volante

Living Room, Private Residence — Milan, Italy — 2015
Vincenzo de Cotiis

Child's Bedroom, A Slow Designed Home — London, England, UK — 2015
Suzy Hoodless

Child's Room, Upper East Side Brownstone — New York, New York, USA — 2017
Ashley Whittaker Design

Bedroom, Private Residence — Long Island, New York, USA — 2010
Kelly Behun (interior design); Sawyer Berson (architecture)

Bedroom, Peter's House — Copenhagen, Denmark — 2015
Studio David Thulstrup

Child's Bedroom, Skok Residence — Lincoln, Massachusetts, USA — 2018
Mally Skok Design

Living Room, Le Palais Bulles — Théoule-sur-Mer, France — 1993
Patrice Breteau (interior design); Antti Lovag (architecture)

Living Room, Von Teese Residence — Los Angeles, California, USA — 2018
Dita Von Teese

Bedroom, Hannah Cecil Gurney Residence — London, England, UK — 2019
Hannah Cecil Gurney

Living Room, Kips Bay Show House — West Palm Beach, Florida, USA — 2020
Suzanne Kasler Interiors

Garden Room, Jaipur Jewel Apartment — Rajasthan, India — 2010
Liza Bruce and Nicholas Alvis Vega

Salon, Private Apartment, De Gournay Showroom — Paris, France — 2020
India Mahdavi

Bedroom, Fredonia Residence — Los Angeles, California, USA — 2019
Nicolò Bini, LINE Architecture

Library, Upper East Side Apartment — New York, New York, USA — 2013
Steven Gambrel, S.R. Gambrel (interior design); Arcologica Architecture (architecture)

Bedroom and Sitting Room, Hacienda Estate — Los Angeles, California, USA — 2004
Carrie Fisher

Sitting Room, Hamptons Home — Sag Harbor, New York, USA — 2005
Steven Gambrel, S.R. Gambrel

Media Room, Washington Square Park Apartment — New York, New York, USA — 2016
Fawn Galli Interiors

Bedroom, Southampton Residence — Southampton, New York, USA — 2018
Bennett Leifer Interiors

Bedroom, Pierre Apartment — New York, New York, USA — 2012
Atelier AM

Living Room, West Village Residence — New York, New York, USA — 2016
Eric Pike and Stefan Steil

Media Room, Palm Beach Residence — Palm Beach, Florida, USA — 2016
Bunny Williams

Living Room, Wallaroy Road Residence — Sydney, New South Wales, Australia — 2016
Tamsin Johnson

Bedroom, Le Palais Bulles — Théoule-sur-Mer, France — 1993
Patrice Breteau (interior design); Antti Lovag (architecture)

Living Room, Midtown Apartment — New York, New York, USA — 2014
Muriel Brandolini

Living Room, West Village Townhouse — New York, New York, USA — 2007
Steven Gambrel, S.R. Gambrel

Guest Room, Chesapeake Residence — Baltimore, Maryland, USA — 2018
Laura Hodges Studio

Living Room, Private Residence — Fayetteville, Arkansas, USA — 2009
Tobi Fairley Interior Design

Dining Room, Captiva Island Residence — Captiva Island, Florida, USA — 2008
Anthony Baratta

Living Room, New Jersey Residence — Summit, New Jersey, USA — 2016
Redd Kaihoi

Bedroom, Château Fourcas-Hosten — Bordeaux, France — 2013
Michael Coorengel and Jean-Pierre Calvagrac

Dining Room, Alhambra Residence — Jacksonville, Florida, USA — 2019
Andrew Howard Interior Design

Living Room, Southampton Residence — Southampton, New York, USA — 2013
Bunny Williams

Living Room, Greenwich Village Residence — New York, New York, USA — 2018
Steven Gambrel, S.R. Gambrel (interior design); HS Jessup (architecture)

Entrance, Franklin Lakes Residence — Franklin Lakes, New Jersey, USA — 2013
Katie Ridder

Dining Room, Revivalist Mansion — Chicago, Illinois, USA — 2019
Steven Gambrel, S.R. Gambrel (interior design); Liederbach & Graham (architecture)

Family Room, Captiva Island Residence — Captiva Island, Florida, USA — 2008
Anthony Baratta

Sitting Room, Birch Castle — San Francisco, California, USA — 2014
Ken Fulk

Dining Room, Birch Castle — San Francisco, California, USA — 2014
Ken Fulk

Breakfast Room, Sarise and Stephen Dweck Residence — Jersey Shore, New Jersey, USA — 2008
Stephen Dweck

Living Room, Macpherson Residence — Miami, Florida, USA — 2019
Sawyer Berson

Dining Room and Kitchen, Asolo Residence — Asolo, Italy — 2018
Michela Goldschmied

Sitting Room, The Lake House — Sonoma, California, USA — 2018
Ken Fulk

Bedroom, Fazenda Guariroba Residence — Campinas, São Paulo, Brazil — 2015
Sig Bergamin

Home Office, Watch Hill Residence — Westerly, Rhode Island, USA — 2018
Studio Giancarlo Valle

Home Office, Family Townhouse — Chicago, Illinois, USA — 2016
Steven Gambrel, S.R. Gambrel (interior design); Liederbach & Graham (architecture)

Dining Room, Fredonia Residence — Los Angeles, California, USA — 2019
Nicolò Bini, LINE Architecture

Library, São Paulo Residence — São Paulo, Brazil — 2017
Sig Bergamin

Sitting Room, Malvern Residence — Melbourne, Victoria, Australia — 2019
Doherty Design Studio

Living Room, Manhattan Penthouse — New York, New York, USA — 2020
Hutton Wilkinson, Tony Duquette

Family Room, Captiva Island Residence — Captiva Island, Florida, USA — 2008
Anthony Baratta

Living Room, Maison Cascades — Saint-Saturnin-lès-Apt, France — 2004
Olivier Massart

Bathroom, Casa Corbellini-Wassermann — Milan, Italy — 2019
Piero Portaluppi (interior design); Studio Binocle (restoration); Antonio Citterio (architecture)

Living and Dining Room, The Beldi Loft Apartment — London, England, UK — 2018
Chan and Eayrs Architects

Garden Room, Creole Cottage — New Orleans, Louisiana, USA — 2010
Carl Palasota

Garden Room, Creole Cottage — New Orleans, Louisiana, USA — 2010
Carl Palasota

Living Room, Park Slope Townhouse — Brooklyn, New York, USA — 2015
James Aguiar and Mark Haldeman

Living Room, A Home for Bella — London, England, UK — 2019
Retrouvius

Salon, Château de Montigny — Normandy, France — 1999
Andrew Allfree

Dining Room, Central Park Residence — New York, New York, USA — 2019
Nicole Fuller Interiors

Living Room, The Harrison — San Francisco, California, USA — 2016
Ken Fulk

Garden, Hopper House — Los Angeles, California, USA — 2018
Martyn Lawrence Bullard

Library, Château Fourcas-Hosten — Bordeaux, France — 2013
Michael Coorengel and Jean-Pierre Calvagrac

Living Room, Arrowhead Farm Cottage — Long Island, New York, USA — 2000
James Morgan Topping

Bedroom, Private Residence — Milan, Italy — 2017
Dimorestudio

Dining Room, House in Tokyo — Tokyo, Japan — 2009
Mlinaric, Henry & Zervudachi (interior design); Kengo Kuma (architecture)

Living Room, Villa D — Marrakech, Morocco — 2004
Studio KO

Bedroom, Ski Chalet — Montana, USA — 2018
Kylee Shintaffer

Living Room, Avalon Vista Residence — Newport Coast, California, USA — 2012
Craig Higgins

Entrance, California Crafstman Home — Palo Alto, California, USA — 2013
DLC-ID de la Cruz Interior Design

Bar, Urban Residence — San Francisco, California, USA — 2018
Martin Kobus, Kobus Interiors

Living Room, San Antonio Factory — San Antonio, Texas, USA — 2010
Gwynn Griffith

Bedroom, Tuscan Guesthouse — Arezzo, Italy — 2012
Roberto Baciocchi

Bedroom, Ett Hem Hotel — Stockholm, Sweden — 2012
Studioilse

Sitting Room, Renwick Residence — New York, New York, USA — 2016
Eran Chen and Ryoko Okada, ODA

Bar, Barwon River House — Melbourne, Victoria, Australia — 2017
Greg Natale

Study, Clinton Hill Brownstone — Brooklyn, New York, USA — 2015
Bespoke Only (interior design), Sarah Jacoby (architecture)

Home Office, Private Residence — Los Angeles, California, USA — 2019
William Hefner

Living Room, Alhadeff and Duzansky Residence — New York, New York, USA — 2017
David Alhadeff, The Future Perfect

Bedroom, West Village Townhouse — New York, New York, USA — 2013
Shawn Henderson Interior Design

Entrance, Medina Riad — Tangier, Morocco — 2007
Roberto Peregalli and Laura Sartori Rimini, Studio Peregalli

Living Room, At Home — Oslo, Norway — 2017
Studio Kråkvik & D'Orazio

Living and Dining Room, Manhattan Pied-à-terre — New York, New York, USA — 2020
Sarah Jacoby Architect

Living Room, Beach Ryosha Residence — Del Mar, California, USA — 2020
Lucas Interior

Entrance, Fitzroy House — Melbourne, Victoria, Australia — 2016
Fiona Lynch Interior Design

Entrance, Highline Residence — New York, New York, USA — 2019
Charles Allem, C.A.D. International

218

DIRECTORY OF DESIGNERS

222

DIRECTORY OF LOCATIONS

226

INDEX

230

ACKNOWLEDGMENTS AND PICTURE CREDITS

231

BIOGRAPHIES

DIRECTORY OF DESIGNERS

A

Cindy Adams
98, Park Avenue Apartment, New York, USA

James Aguiar and Mark Haldeman
177, Park Slope Townhouse, Brooklyn, USA

David Alhadeff
206, Alhadeff and Duzansky Residence, New York, USA

Alidad
72, Parisian Pied-a-terre, Paris, France

Charles Allem
215, Highline Residence, New York, USA

Andrew Allfree
83, 182, Château de Montigny, Normandy, France

Michelle Andrews
21, Lakeside House, Wayzata, USA

Atelier AM
132, Pierre Apartment, New York, USA

B

Roberto Baciocchi
200, Tuscan Guesthouse, Arezzo, Italy

Anthony Baratta
142, 150, 168, Captiva Island Residence, Captiva Island, USA

Kelly Behun
114, Private Residence, Long Island, USA

Sig Bergamin
58, 157, Fazenda Guariroba Residence, Campinas, Brazil
163, São Paulo Residence, São Paulo, Brazil

Bespoke Only
204, Clinton Hill Brownstone, Brooklyn, USA

Frank de Biasi and Gene Meyer
166, Park Avenue Residence, New York, USA

Bruce Bierman
128, Chelsea Loft, New York, USA

Nicolò Bini
124, 162, Fredonia Residence, Los Angeles, USA

Steve Blatz
18, 19, Art Dealer's Loft, Long Island City, USA

BNO Design
107, Wine Beach Residence, Rockaway Park, USA

Piet Boon
25, Townhouse, New York, USA

Christian Boros
34, Penthouse Bunker, Berlin, Germany

Melissa Bowers
40, Reflections Residence, New York, USA

Alessandra Branca
174, Townhouse, Chicago, USA

Muriel Brandolini
137, Midtown Apartment, New York, USA

Patrice Breteau
117, 136, Le Palais Bulles, Théoule-sur-Mer, France

Thomas Britt
92, 93, Pied-à-terre, San Francisco, USA

Liza Bruce and Nicholas Alvis Vega
102, 122, Jaipur Jewel Apartment, Rajasthan, India

Martyn Lawrence Bullard
38, Hidden Ridge Residence, Hidden Hills, USA
181, Villa Grigio, Palm Springs, USA
185, Hopper House, Los Angeles, USA

Patricia Bustos
106, Minimal Fantasy Apartment, Madrid, Spain

C

Thomas Callaway
87, Spanish Colonial Revival House, Los Angeles, USA

Rafael de Cárdenas
30, Greenwich Village Residence, New York, USA
33, Belnord Apartment, New York, USA

Hannah Cecil Gurney
119, Hannah Cecil Gurney Residence, London, UK

Chan and Eayrs Architects
171, The Beldi Loft Apartment, London, UK

Eran Chen and Ryoko Okada
202, Renwick Residence, New York, USA

Clary Collection
178, The Ensworth, Nashville, USA

Anthony Collett
56, London House, London, UK

Michael Coorengel and Jean-Pierre Calvagrac
50, 144, 186, Château Fourcas-Hosten, Bordeaux, France

Robert Couturier
79, Fifth Avenue Apartment, New York, USA

Cullman & Kravis
51, New Jersey Country Home, New Jersey, USA

D

Studio Daminato
60, MJ Residence, Undisclosed Location
64, Pool House, Villa Peduzzi, Lake Como, Italy

Vincenzo de Cotiis
111, Private Residence, Milan, Italy

Dekar Design
20, Peach Farm Residence, East Hampton, USA

Barbara Dente
16, New York City Apartment, New York, USA

Benjamin Dhong
48, Woodside Residence, Woodside, USA

Dimorestudio
189, Private Residence, Milan, Italy

Joseph Dirand
27, Private Residence, Frankfurt, Germany
28, Avenue Montaigne Apartment, Paris, France

DLC-ID de la Cruz Interior Design
196, California Craftsman Home, Palo Alto, USA

Doherty Design Studio
19, St Kilda Residence, Melbourne, Australia
64, Malvern Residence, Melbourne, Australia

Mary Douglas Drysdale
45, Georgetown Cottage, Washington, USA

Stephen Dweck
90, 153, Sarise and Stephen Dweck Residence, Jersey Shore, USA

Jenny Dyer
32, Manhattan Apartment, New York, USA

E

Jorge Elias
59, 80, Elias Residence, São Paulo, Brazil

Pedro Espírito Santo
47, Pedro Espírito Santo Residence, Lisbon, Portugal

F

Tobi Fairley
141, Private Residence, Fayetteville, USA

Solveig Fernlund and Neil Logan
23, Lafayette Street Residence, New York, USA

Carrie Fisher
126, Hacienda Estate, Los Angeles, USA

Ken Fulk
67, Sky High Residence, Yellowstone, USA
69, Provincetown Residence, Provincetown, USA
105, Private Residence, Cabo San Lucas, Mexico
151, 152, Birch Castle, San Francisco, USA
156, The Lake House, Sonoma, USA
180, Kips Bay Show House, New York, USA
184, The Harrison, San Francisco, USA
187, Monkey Inferno, San Francisco, USA
193, Cypress Grove, San Francisco, USA

Nicole Fuller
183, Central Park Residence, New York, USA

G

Fawn Galli
129, Washington Square Park Apartment, New York, USA

Steven Gambrel
89, 149, Revivalist Mansion, Chicago, USA
91, Palmolive Apartment, Chicago, USA
125, Upper East Side Apartment, New York, USA
127, Hamptons Home, Sag Harbor, USA
138, 139, West Village Townhouse, New York, USA
147, Greenwich Village Residence, New York, USA
158, 161, Family Townhouse, Chicago, USA

Golden
22, Brighton Residence, Brighton, Australia

Michela Goldschmied
101, 155, Asolo Residence, Asolo, Italy

Gwynn Griffith
199, San Antonio Factory, San Antonio, USA

Grisanti & Cussen
70, Casa Foa, Santiago, Chile

H

William Hefner
205, Private Residence, Los Angeles, USA

Shawn Henderson
208, West Village Townhouse, New York, USA

Craig Higgins
194, Avalon Vista Residence, Newport Coast, USA

Laura Hodges
140, Chesapeake Residence, Baltimore, USA

Suzy Hoodless
112, A Slow Designed Home, London, UK

Andrew Howard
145, Alhambra Residence, Jacksonville, USA

I

Anthony Ingrao
103, Richard and Lisa Perry Penthouse, New York, USA

J

Sarah Jacoby
211, Manhattan Pied-à-terre, New York, USA

Jay Jeffers
85, Private Residence, New York, USA

Betsey Johnson
52, Betsey Johnson Residence, Malibu, USA

Tamsin Johnson
135, Wallaroy Road Residence, Sydney, Australia

Christina Juarez
78, Juarez and Ploener Residence, New York, USA

K

Suzanne Kasler
44, Buckhead Residence, Atlanta, USA
120, Kips Bay Show House, West Palm Beach, USA

Martin Kobus
198, Urban Residence, San Francisco, USA

Studio Kråkvik & D'Orazio
210, At Home, Oslo, Norway

Kravitz Design in collaboration with Disco Volante
110, Williams Residence, Beverly Hills, USA

L

Bennett Leifer
131, Southampton Residence, Southampton, USA

LOT-EK
77, Irving Place Carriage House, Brooklyn, USA

Lucas Interior
213, Beach Ryosha Residence, Del Mar, USA

Fiona Lynch
214, Fitzroy House, Melbourne, Australia

M

India Mahdavi
123, De Gournay Showroom, Paris, France

Peter Marino
71, Ski Retreat, Rocky Mountains, USA

Olivier Massart
169, Maison Cascades, Saint-Saturnin-lès-Apt, France

Mlinaric, Henry & Zervudachi
190, House in Tokyo, Tokyo, Japan

Janie Molster
81, Molster Residence, Richmond, USA

Juan Pablo Molyneux
75, Pebble Beach Residence, Monterey, USA

Juan Montoya
55, Cap Cana Residence, Cap Cana, Dominican Republic

Wesley Moon
35, Xanadune Residence, Southampton, USA

N

Greg Natale
96, 97, Darlinghurst Apartment, Sydney, Australia
203, 207, Barwon River House, Melbourne, Australia

Norm Architects
197, The Audo, Copenhagen, Denmark

P

Carl Palasota
172, 173, 176, Creole Cottage, New Orleans, USA

John Peixinho
66, The Old Red Schoolhouse, Middletown, USA

Roberto Peregalli and Laura Sartori Rimini
62, Hotel Particulier Apartment, Paris, France
209, Medina Riad, Tangier, Morocco

Thomas Pheasant
31, 42, Park Avenue Apartment, New York, USA

Eric Pike and Stefan Steil
133, West Village Residence, New York, USA

Piero Portaluppi
170, Casa Corbellini-Wassermann, Milan, Italy

Ann Pyne
43, 88, New York City Townhouse, New York, USA
46, Southampton Cottage, Southampton, USA

R

Karim Rashid
104, Chelsea Loft, Rashid Residence, New York, USA

Reath Design
86, Franklin Hills Residence, Los Angeles, USA

Redd Kaihoi
53, 94, Houston Residence Houston, USA
143, New Jersey Residence, Summit, USA
159, Vacation Home, Bellville, USA
167, Bay Area Residence, San Francisco, USA

Retrouvius
61, A Country Home in the City, London, UK
179, A Home for Bella, London, UK

Richards Stanisich
109, Beach House, Sydney, Australia

Katie Ridder
148, Franklin Lakes Residence, Franklin Lakes, USA

Valerian Rybar
175, Beaulieu, Newport, USA

S

Achille Salvagni
95, Achille Salvagni Atelier, London, UK

Stephen Samuelson
84, 100, Trey Trust Residence, Los Angeles, USA

Laura Santos
76, Manhattan Townhouse, New York, USA

Sawyer Berson
154, Macpherson Residence, Miami, USA

Kathryn Scott
82, Brooklyn Heights Townhouse, Brooklyn, USA

Pamela Shamshiri
65, Lechner House, Los Angeles, USA

SheltonMindel
41, Miami Beach Oceanfront Residence, Miami, USA

Kylee Shintaffer
192, Ski Chalet, Montana, USA

Stephen Sills
130, Connecticut Saltbox, Connecticut, USA

Mally Skok
116, Skok Residence, Lincoln, USA

Snarkitecture
26, Studio, Brooklyn, USA
68, Daniel Arsham Residence, Long Island, USA

Sara Story
39, Bel Air Residence, Los Angeles, USA

Studioilse
37, Palau de Casavells, Galeria Miquel Azueta, El Baix Empordà, Spain
195, 201, Ett Hem Hotel, Stockholm, Sweden

Studio KO
191, Villa D, Marrakech, Morocco

T

Studio David Thulstrup
36, Vester Voldgade Residence, Copenhagen, Denmark
115, Peter's House, Copenhagen, Denmark

Faye Toogood
29, North Hill Residence, London, UK
212, Tapestry Penthouse, London, UK

James Morgan Topping
188, Arrowhead Farm Cottage, Long Island, USA

Michael Trapp
54, The Farm, Sharon, USA

V

Giancarlo Valle
160, Watch Hill Residence, Westerly, USA

Alberto Villalobos
74, Arnell Residence, Katonah, USA

Dita Von Teese
24, 118, Von Teese Residence, Los Angeles, USA

W

Kelly Wearstler
49, 63, Malibu Residence, Malibu, USA
57, Bellagio Residence, Los Angeles, USA
73, Madison Avenue Residence, New York, USA

Ashley Whittaker
113, Upper East Side Brownstone, New York, USA

Hutton Wilkinson, Tony Duquette
165, Manhattan Penthouse, New York, USA

Bunny Williams
108, 134, Palm Beach Residence, Palm Beach, USA
121, 146, Southampton Residence, Southampton, USA

Workshop/APD
17, Panoramic Penthouse, New York, USA

DIRECTORY OF LOCATIONS

AUSTRALIA

Doherty Design Studio
99, St Kilda Residence, Melbourne
164, Malvern Residence, Melbourne

Golden
22, Brighton Residence, Brighton

Tamsin Johnson
135, Wallaroy Road Residence, Sydney

Fiona Lynch
214, Fitzroy House, Melbourne

Greg Natale
96, 97, Darlinghurst Apartment, Sydney
203, 207, Barwon River House, Melbourne

Richards Stanisich
109, Beach House, Sydney

BRAZIL

Sig Bergamin
58, 157, Fazenda Guariroba Residence, Campinas
163, São Paulo Residence, São Paulo

Jorge Elias
59, 80, Elias Residence, São Paulo

CHILE

Grisanti & Cussen
70, Casa Foa, Santiago

DENMARK

Norm Architects
197, The Audo, Copenhagen

Studio David Thulstrup
36, Vester Voldgade Residence, Copenhagen
115, Peter's House, Copenhagen

DOMINICAN REPUBLIC

Juan Montoya
55, Cap Cana Residence, Cap Cana

FRANCE

Alidad
72, Parisian Pied-à-terre, Paris

Andrew Allfree
83, 182, Château de Montigny, Normandy

Patrice Breteau
117, 136, Le Palais Bulles, Théoule-sur-Mer

Michael Coorengel and Jean-Pierre Calvagrac
50, 144, 186, Château Fourcas-Hosten, Bordeaux

Joseph Dirand
28, Avenue Montaigne Apartment, Paris

Roberto Peregalli and Laura Sartori Rimini
62, Hotel Particulier Apartment, Paris

India Mahdavi
123, De Gournay Showroom, Paris

Olivier Massart
169, Maison Cascades, Saint-Saturnin-lès-Apt

GERMANY

Christian Boros
34, Penthouse Bunker, Berlin

Joseph Dirand
27, Private Residence, Frankfurt

INDIA

Liza Bruce and Nicholas Alvis Vega
102, 122, Jaipur Jewel Apartment, Rajasthan

ITALY

Roberto Baciocchi
200, Tuscan Guesthouse, Arezzo

Studio Daminato
64, Pool House, Villa Peduzzi, Lake Como

Vincenzo de Cotiis
111, Private Residence, Milan

Dimorestudio
189, Private Residence, Milan

Michela Goldschmied
101, 155, Asolo Residence, Asolo

Piero Portaluppi
170, Casa Corbellini-Wassermann, Milan

JAPAN

Mlinaric, Henry & Zervudachi
190, House in Tokyo, Tokyo

MEXICO

Ken Fulk
105, Private Residence, Cabo San Lucas

MOROCCO

Studio KO
191, Villa D, Marrakech

Roberto Peregalli and Laura Sartori Rimini
209, Medina Riad, Tangier

NORWAY

Studio Kråkvik & D'Orazio
210, At Home, Oslo

PORTUGAL

Pedro Espírito Santo
47, Pedro Espírito Santo Residence, Lisbon

SPAIN

Patricia Bustos Studio
106, Minimal Fantasy Apartment, Madrid

Studioilse
37, Palau de Casavells, Galeria Miquel Azueta, El Baix Empordà

SWEDEN

Studioilse
195, 201, Ett Hem Hotel, Stockholm

UK

Hannah Cecil Gurney
119, Hannah Cecil Gurney Residence, London

Chan and Eayrs Architects
171, The Beldi Loft Apartment, London

Anthony Collett
56, London House, London

Suzy Hoodless
112, A Slow Designed Home, London

Retrouvius
161, A Country Home in the City, London
179, A Home for Bella, London

Achille Salvagni
95, Achille Salvagni Atelier, London

Faye Toogood
99, North Hill Residence, London
212, Tapestry Penthouse, London

USA

Cindy Adams
8, Park Avenue Apartment, New York

James Aguiar and Mark Haldeman
177, Park Slope Townhouse, Brooklyn

David Alhadeff
206, Alhadeff and Duzansky Residence, New York

Charles Allem
215, Highline Residence, New York

Michelle Andrews
21, Lakeside House, Wayzata

Atelier AM
132, Pierre Apartment, New York

Anthony Baratta
142, 150, 168, Captiva Island Residence, Captiva Island

Kelly Behun
114, Private Residence, Long Island

Sawyer Berson
154, Macpherson Residence, Miami

Bespoke Only
204, Clinton Hill Brownstone, Brooklyn

Frank de Biasi and Gene Meyer
166, Park Avenue Residence, New York

Bruce Bierman
128, Chelsea Loft, New York

Nicolò Bini
124, 162, Fredonia Residence, Los Angeles

Steve Blatz
18, 19, Art Dealer's Loft, Long Island City

BNO Design
107, Wine Beach Residence, Rockaway Park

Piet Boon
25, Townhouse, New York

Melissa Bowers
40, Reflections Residence, New York

Alessandra Branca
174, Townhouse, Chicago

Muriel Brandolini
137, Midtown Apartment, New York

Thomas Britt
92, 93, Pied-à-terre, San Francisco

Martyn Lawrence Bullard
38, Hidden Ridge Residence, Hidden Hills
181, Villa Grigio, Palm Springs
185, Hopper House, Los Angeles

Thomas Callaway
87, Spanish Colonial Revival House, Los Angeles

Rafael de Cárdenas
30, Greenwich Village Residence, New York
33, Belnord Apartment, New York

Eran Chen and Ryoko Okada
202, Renwick Residence, New York

Clary Collection
178, The Ensworth, Nashville

Robert Couturier
79, Fifth Avenue Apartment, New York

Cullman & Kravis
51, New Jersey Country Home, New Jersey

Dekar Design
20, Peach Farm Residence, East Hampton

Barbara Dente
16, New York City Apartment, New York

Benjamin Dhong
48, Woodside Residence, Woodside

DLC-ID de la Cruz Interior Design
196, California Craftsman Home, Palo Alto

Mary Douglas Drysdale
45, Georgetown Cottage, Washington

Stephen Dweck
90, 153, Sarise and Stephen Dweck Residence, Jersey Shore

Jenny Dyer
32, Manhattan Apartment, New York

Tobi Fairley
141, Private Residence, Fayetteville

Solveig Fernlund and Neil Logan
23, Lafayette Street Residence, New York

Carrie Fisher
126, Hacienda Estate, Los Angeles

Ken Fulk
67, Sky High Residence, Yellowstone
69, Provincetown Residence, Provincetown
151, 152, Birch Castle, San Francisco
156, The Lake House, Sonoma
180, Kips Bay Show House, New York
184, The Harrison, San Francisco
187, Monkey Inferno, San Francisco
193, Cypress Grove, San Francisco

Nicole Fuller
183, Central Park Residence, New York

Fawn Galli
129, Washington Square Park Apartment, New York

Steven Gambrel
89, 149, Revivalist Mansion, Chicago
91, Palmolive Apartment, Chicago
125, Upper East Side Apartment, New York
127, Hamptons Home, Sag Harbor
138, 139, West Village Townhouse, New York
147, Greenwich Village Residence, New York
158, 161, Family Townhouse, Chicago

Gwynn Griffith
199, San Antonio Factory, San Antonio

William Hefner
205, Private Residence, Los Angeles

Shawn Henderson
208, West Village Townhouse, New York

Craig Higgins
194, Avalon Vista Residence, Newport Coast

Laura Hodges
140, Chesapeake Residence, Baltimore

Andrew Howard
145, Alhambra Residence, Jacksonville

Anthony Ingrao
103, Richard and Lisa Perry Penthouse, New York

Sarah Jacoby
211, Manhattan Pied-à-terre, New York

Jay Jeffers
85, Private Residence, New York

Betsey Johnson
52, Betsey Johnson Residence, Malibu

Christina Juarez
78, Juarez and Ploener Residence, New York

Suzanne Kasler
44, Buckhead Residence, Atlanta
120, Kips Bay Show House, West Palm Beach

Martin Kobus
198, Urban Residence, San Francisco

Kravitz Design in collaboration with Disco Volante
110, Williams Residence, Beverly Hills

Bennett Leifer
131, Southampton Residence, Southampton

LOT-EK
77, Irving Place Carriage House, Brooklyn

Lucas Interior
213, Beach Ryosha Residence, Del Mar

Peter Marino
71, Ski Retreat, Rocky Mountains

Janie Molster
81, Molster Residence, Richmond

Juan Pablo Molyneux
75, Pebble Beach Residence, Monterey

Wesley Moon
35, Xanadune Residence, Southampton

Carl Palasota
172, 173, 176, Creole Cottage, New Orleans

John Peixinho
66, The Old Red Schoolhouse, Middletown

Thomas Pheasant
31, 42, Park Avenue Apartment, New York

Eric Pike and Stefan Steil
133, West Village Residence, New York

Ann Pyne
43, 88 New York City Townhouse, New York
46, Southampton Cottage Southampton

Karim Rashid
104, Chelsea Loft, Rashid Residence, New York

Reath Design
86, Franklin Hills Residence, Los Angeles

Redd Kaihoi
53, 94, Houston Residence, Houston
143, New Jersey Residence, Summit
159, Vacation Home, Bellville
167, Bay Area Residence, San Francisco

Katie Ridder
148, Franklin Lakes Residence, Franklin Lakes

Valerian Rybar
175, Beaulieu, Newport

Stephen Samuelson
84, 100, Trey Trust Residence, Los Angeles

Laura Santos
78, Manhattan Townhouse, New York

Kathryn Scott
82, Brooklyn Heights Townhouse, Brooklyn

Pamela Shamshiri
65, Lechner House, Los Angeles

Kylee Shintaffer
192, Ski Chalet, Montana

Mally Skok
116, Skok Residence, Lincoln

SheltonMindel
41, Miami Beach Oceanfront Residence, Miami Beach

Stephen Sills
130, Connecticut Saltbox, Connecticut

Snarkitecture
26, Studio, Brooklyn
68, Daniel Arsham Residence, Long Island

Sara Story
39, Bel Air Residence, Los Angeles

James Morgan Topping
188, Arrowhead Farm Cottage, Long Island

Michael Trapp
54, The Farm, Sharon

Giancarlo Valle
160, Watch Hill Residence, Westerly

Alberto Villalobos
74, Arnell Residence, Katonah

Dita Von Teese
24, 118, Von Teese Residence, Los Angeles

Kelly Wearstler
49, 63, Malibu Residence, Malibu
57, Bellagio Residence, Los Angeles
73, Madison Avenue Residence, New York

Ashley Whittaker
113, Upper East Side Brownstone, New York

Bunny Williams
108, 134, Palm Beach Residence, Palm Beach
121, 146, Southampton Residence, Southampton

Hutton Wilkinson, Tony Duquette
165, Manhattan Penthouse, New York

Workshop/APD
17, Panoramic Penthouse, New York

Undisclosed
Studio Daminato
60, MJ Residence, Undisclosed Location

INDEX

A

Achille Salvagni Atelier, London *95*
Adams, Cindy *98*
Aguiar, James *177*
Albers, Josef *7, 9*
Alhadeff, David *206*
Alhadeff and Duzansky Residence, New York *206*
Alhambra Residence, Jacksonville *145*
Alidad *72*
Allem, Charles *215*
Allfree, Andrew *83, 182*
Andrew Howard Interior Design *145*
Andrews, Michelle *21*
Arcologica Architecture *125*
Aristotle *7*
Arnell Residence, Katonah *74*
Arrowhead Farm Cottage, Long Island *188*
Art Dealer's Loft, Long Island City *18, 19*
Ashley Whittaker Design *113*
Asolo Residence *101, 155*
At Home, Oslo *210*
Atelier AM *132*
The Audo, Copenhagen *197*
Avalon Vista Residence, Newport *194*
Avenue Montaigne Apartment, Paris *28*

B

Babylonians *10*
Baciocchi, Roberto *200*
Baratta, Anthony *142, 150, 168*
Barwon River House, Melbourne *203, 207*
Bay Area Residence, San Francisco *167*
Beach House, Sydney *109*
Beach Ryosha Residence, Del Mar *213*
Beaulieu, Newport *175*
Behun, Kelly *114*
Bel Air Residence, Los Angeles *39*
The Beldi Loft Apartment, London *171*
Bellagio Residence, Los Angeles *57*
Belnord Apartment, New York *33*
Bennett Leifer Interiors *131*
Bergamin, Sig
 Fazenda Guariroba Residence *58, 157*
 São Paulo Residence *163*
Berson, Sawyer *114, 154*
Bespoke Only *204*
Betsey Johnson Residence, Malibu *52*
Biasi, Frank de *166*
Bini, Nicolò *124, 162*
Birch Castle, San Francisco *151, 152*
Blatz, Steve *18, 19*
BNO Design *107*
Boros, Christian *34*
Bowers, M.A. *40*
Branca, Alessandra *174*
Brandolini, Muriel *137*
Breteau, Patrice *117, 136*
Brighton Residence *22*
Britt, Thomas *92, 93*
Brooklyn Heights Townhouse *82*
Bruce, Liza *102, 122*
Bruce Bierman Design *128*
Buckhead Residence, Atlanta *44*
Bullard, Martyn Lawrence
 Hidden Ridge Residence *38*
 Hopper House *185*
 Villa Grigio *181*

C

C.A.D. International *215*
California Craftsman Home, Palo Alto *196*
Callaway, Thomas *87*
Calvagrac, Jean-Pierre *50, 144, 186*
Cap Cana Residence *55*
Captiva Island Residence *142, 150, 168*
Cárdenas, Rafael de *30, 33*
Casa Corbellini-Wassermann, Milan *170*
Casa Foa, Santiago *70*
Central Park Residence, New York *183*
Chan and Eayrs Architects *171*
Château de Montigny, Normandy *83, 182*
Château Fourcas-Hosten, Bordeaux *50, 144, 186*
Chelsea Loft, New York *128*
Chelsea Loft, Rashid Residence, New York *104*
Chen, Eran *202*
Chesapeake Residence, Baltimore *140*
Christina Juarez and Company *78*
C.I.E. (Commission International de l'Éclairage) *9*
Citterio, Antonio *170*
Clary Collection *178*
Clinton Hill Brownstone, Brooklyn *204*
Collett, Anthony *56*
Condesa, Mexico City *13*
Connecticut Saltbox, Connecticut *130*
Coorengel, Michael *50, 144, 186*
A Country Home in the City, London *61*
Couturier, Robert *79*
Creole Cottage, New Orleans *172, 173, 176*
Cullman & Kravis *51*
Cypress Grove, San Francisco *193*

D

Daniel Arsham Residence, Long Island *68*
Darlinghurst Apartment, Sydney *96, 97*
Darwin, Charles *12*
De Cotiis, Vincenzo *111*
Dekar Design *20*
Dente, Barbara *16*
Dhong, Benjamin *48*
Diebenkorn, Richard *8*
Dimorestudio *189*
Dirand, Joseph *27, 28*
Disco Volante *110*
DLC-ID de la Cruz Interior Design *196*
Doherty Design Studio *99, 164*
Drysdale, Mary Douglas *45*
Duquette, Tony *165*
Dweck, Stephen *90, 153*
Dyer, Jenny *32*

E

Egyptians, ancient *10*
Elias, Jorge *59, 80*

Elias Residence, São
    Paulo 59, 80
The Ensworth, Nashville
    178
Ett Hem Hotel, Stockholm
    195, 201

F

Family Townhouse,
    Chicago 158, 161
The Farm, Sharon 54
Fawn Galli Interiors 129
Fazenda Guariroba
    Residence, Campinas
    58, 157
Fernlund, Solveig 23
Fifth Avenue Apartment,
    New York 79
Fiona Lynch Interior
    Design 214
Fisher, Carrie 126
Fitzroy House, Melbourne
    214
Franklin Hills Residence,
    Los Angeles 86
Franklin Lakes Residence
    148
Fredonia Residence,
    Los Angeles 124, 162
Freud, Lucian 8
Frey, Pierre 13
Fulk, Ken
    Birch Castle 151, 152
    Cypress Grove 193
    The Harrison 184
    Kips Bay Show House
        180
    The Lake House 156
    Monkey Inferno 187
    Private Residence,
        Cabo San Lucas 105
    Provincetown
        Residence 69
    Sky High Residence 67
The Future Perfect 206

G

Gambrel, Steven
    Family Townhouse,
        Chicago 158, 161
    Greenwich Village
        Residence 147
    Hamptons Home 127
    Palmolive Apartment 91
    Revivalist Mansion 89,
        149
    Upper East Side
        Apartment 125
    West Village
        Townhouse 138, 139
Gauguin, Paul 9
Georgetown Cottage,
    Washington 45
Goethe, Johann Wolfgang
    van 7–8
Golden 22
Goldschmied, Michela
    101, 155
Greeks 10
Greenwich Village
    Residence, New York
    30, 147
Griffith, Gwynn 199
Grisanti & Cussen 70
Gurney, Hannah Cecil
    119

H

Hacienda Estate, Los
    Angeles 126
Haldeman, Mark 177
Hamptons Home, Sag
    Harbor 127
Hannah Cecil Gurney
    Residence, London 119
The Harrison, San
    Francisco 184
Hefner, William 205
Hidden Ridge Residence
    38

Higgins, Craig 194
Highline Residence, New
    York 215
A Home for Bella, London
    179
Hoodless, Suzy 112
Hopper House, Los
    Angeles 185
Hotel Particulier
    Apartment, Paris 62
House in Tokyo 190
Houston Residence 53,
    94

I

Ingrao, Anthony 103
Irving Place Carriage
    House, Brooklyn 77

J

J. P. Molyneux Studio 75
Jacoby, Sarah 204
Jaipur Jewel Apartment,
    Rajasthan 102, 122
James Morgan Topping
    188
Jeffers, Jay 85
Jessup, HS 147
Johnson, Betsey 52
Johnson, Tamsin 135
Juan Montoya Design 55
Juarez, Christina 78
Juarez and Ploener
    Residence, New York 78
Jung, Carl 8

K

Kathryn Scott Design
    Studio 82
Kips Bay Show House,
    New York 180
Kips Bay Show House,
    West Palm Beach 120

Kobus, Martin 198
Kobus Interiors 198
Kravitz Design 110
Kuma, Kengo 190

L

Lafayette Street
    Residence, New York
    23
The Lake House, Sonoma
    156
Lakeside House, Wayzata
    21
Laura Hodges Studio
    140
Laura Santos Interiors 76
Le Corbusier 10
Le Palais Bulles, Théoule-
    sur-Mer 117, 136
Lechner House, Los
    Angeles 65
Léger, Fernand 6
Liederbach & Graham
    Family Townhouse,
        Chicago 158, 161
    Palmolive Apartment 91
    Revivalist Mansion 89,
        149
LINE Architecture 124,
    162
Logan, Neil 23
London House 56
LOT-EK 77
Lovag, Antti 117, 136
Lucas Interior 213
Lüscher, Max 8
Lynch, David 13

M

McMillen
    New York City
        Townhouse 43, 88
    Southampton Cottage
        46

Macpherson Residence, Miami 154
Madison Avenue Residence, New York 73
Mahdavi, India 12–13, 123
Maison Cascades, Saint-Saturnin-lès-Apt 169
Malibu Residence 49, 63
Mally Skok Design 116
Malvern Residence, Melbourne 164
Manhattan Apartment, New York 32
Manhattan Penthouse, New York 165
Manhattan Pied-à-terre, New York 211
Manhattan Townhouse, New York 76
Marie Antoinette 10
Marino, Peter 71
Massart, Olivier 169
Mayans 10
Mazouz, Mourad 13
Medina Riad, Tangier 209
Mériguet-Carrère 13
Meyer, Gene 166
Miami Beach Oceanfront Residence 41
Midtown Apartment, New York 137
Minimal Fantasy Apartment, Madrid 106
MJ Residence 60
Mlinaric, Henry & Zervudachi 190
Molster, Janie 81
Molster Residence, Richmond 81
Mondrian, Piet 8
Monkey Inferno, San Francisco 187
Moon, Wesley 35
Munsell, A. H. 9

N

Natale, Greg
Barwon River House 203, 207
Darlinghurst Apartment 96, 97
New Jersey Country Home 51
New Jersey Residence, Summit 143
New York City Apartment, Jean Nouvel Building 16
New York City Townhouse 43, 88
Newton, Isaac 7
Nicole Fuller Interiors 183
Norm Architects 197
North Hill Residence, London 29

O

ODA 202
Okada, Ryoko 202
The Old Red Schoolhouse, Middletown 66

P

Palasota, Carl 172, 173, 176
Palau de Casavelis, Galeria Miquel Azueta, El Baix Gemporà 37
Palm Beach Residence 108, 134
Palmolive Apartment, Chicago 91
Panoramic Penthouse, New York 17
Parisian Pied-à-terre, Paris 72
Park Avenue Apartment, New York 31, 42, 98
Park Avenue Residence, New York 166
Park Slope Townhouse, Brooklyn 177
Patricia Bustos Studio 106
Paul, Stella 6–11
Peach Farm Residence, East Hampton 20
Pebble Beach Residence, Monterrey 75
Pedro Espírito Santo Residence, Lisbon 47
Peixinho, John 66
Penthouse Bunker, Berlin 34
Peregalli, Roberto 62, 209
Peter's House, Copenhagen 115
Pied-à-terre, San Francisco 92, 93
Pierre Apartment, New York 132
Pike, Eric 133
Pirahã 9
Plan A Architecture 84, 100
Pompei 10, 11
Pool House, Villa Peduzzi, Lake Como 64
Portaluppi, Piero 170
Private Apartment, De Gournay Showroom, Paris 123
Private Residence, Cabo San Lucas 105
Private Residence, Fayetteville 141
Private Residence, Frankfurt 27
Private Residence, Long Island 114
Private Residence, Los Angeles 205
Private Residence, Milan 111, 189

Private Residence, New York 85
Provincetown Residence 69
Pyne, Ann
New York City Townhouse 43, 88
Southampton Cottage 46

R

Rashid, Karim 104
Reath Design 86
Redd Kaihoi
Bay Area Residence 167
Houston Residence 53, 94
New Jersey Residence 143
Vacation Home, Bellville 159
Reflections Residence, New York 40
Renaissance Europe 10
Renwick Residence, New York 202
Retrouvius 61, 179
Revivalist Mansion, Chicago 89, 149
Richard and Lisa Perry Penthouse, New York 103
Richards Stanisich 109
Ridder, Katie 148
Rimini, Laura Sartori 62, 209
Romans 10, 11
Rybar, Valerian 175

S

St. Kilda Residence, Melbourne 99
Salvagni, Achille 95

Samuelson, Stephen 84, 100
San Antonio Factory 199
Santo, Pedro Espírito 47
São Paulo Residence 163
Sara Story Design 39
Sarah Jacoby Architect 211
Sarise and Stephen Dweck Residence, Jersey Shore 90, 153
Shamshiri, Pamela 65
Shawn Henderson Interior Design 208
SheltonMindel 41
Shintaffer, Kylee 192
Sketch 13
Ski Chalet, Montana 192
Ski Retreat, Rocky Mountains 71
Skok Residence, Lincoln 116
Sky High Residence, Yellowstone 67
A Slow Designed Home, London 112
Snarkitecture 26, 68
Southampton Cottage 46
Southampton Residence 121, 131, 146
Spanish Colonial Revival House, Los Angeles 87
S.R. Gambrel
  Family Townhouse, Chicago 158, 161
  Greenwich Village Residence 147
  Hamptons Home 127
  Palmolive Apartment 91
  Revivalist Mansion 89, 149
  Upper East Side Apartment 125
  West Village Townhouse 138, 139
Steil, Stefan 133

Stein, Gertrude 10
Stephen Sills Associates 130
Studio, Brooklyn 26
Studio Binocle 170
Studio Daminato 60, 64
Studio David Thulstrup 36, 115
Studio Giancarlo Valle 160
Studio KO 191
Studio Kråkvik & D'Orazio 210
Studio Peregalli 62, 209
Studio Piet Boon 25
Studioilse
  Ett Hem Hotel 195, 201
  Palau de Casavelis, Galeria Miquel Azueta 37
Suzanne Kasler Interiors 44, 120

T

Tapestry Penthouse, London 212
Thomas Pheasant Studio 31, 42
Tobi Fairley Interior Design 141
Toogood, Faye 29, 212
Townhouse, Chicago 174
Townhouse, New York 25
Trapp, Michael 54
Trey Trust Residence, Los Angeles 84, 100
Tuscan Guesthouse, Arezzo 200

U

Upper East Side Apartment, New York 125

Upper East Side Brownstone, New York 113
Urban Residence, San Francisco 198

V

Vacation House, Bellville 159
Vega, Nicholas Alvis 102, 122
Vester Voldgade Residence, Copenhagen 36
Villa D, Marrakech 191
Villa Grigio, Palm Springs 181
Villalobos, Alberto 74
Von Teese, Dita 24, 118
Von Teese Residence, Los Angeles 24, 118

W

Wallaroy Road Residence, Sydney 135
Washington Square Park Apartment, New York 129
Watch Hill Residence, Westerly 160
Wearstler, Kelly
  Bellagio Residence 57
  Madison Avenue Residence 73
  Malibu Residence 49, 63
West Village Residence, New York 133
West Village Townhouse, New York 138, 139, 208
Wilkinson, Hutton 165
Williams, Bunny
  Palm Beach Residence 108, 134

Southampton Residence 121, 146
Williams Residence, Beverly Hills 110
Wine Beach Residence, Rockaway Park 107
Woodside Residence, Woodside 48
Workshop/APD 17

X

Xanadune Residence, Southampton 35

ACKNOWLEDGMENTS AND PICTURE CREDITS

PUBLISHER'S ACKNOWLEDGMENTS

The publisher would like to acknowledge the invaluable contributions of the following people, without whom this book would not have been possible. Tim Balaam, Vanessa Bird, Clive Burroughs, Julia Hasting, Melissa LeBoeuf, India Mahdavi, João Mota, Anthony Naughton, Celeste Ollivier, Stella Paul, Holly Pollard, Kate Sclater, Kim Scott, Hans Strofregen, and Anthony Tran.

PICTURE CREDITS

Note: On page 205, the artwork shown above the fireplace in the home of the founder of Design Gallery Galerie Provenance is a 1937 lithography by artist Benjamin Abramowitz. © Peter Aaron/OTTO: 103; © Brittany Ambridge/OTTO: 20; Photography by Irina Boersma, courtesy of David Thulstrup: 36; Photography by Henry Bourne, courtesy of Toogood: 29; Dave Brook: 112; Sharyn Cairns: 22, 214; Pascal Chevallier: 62; Justin Coit/Trunk Archive: 52; © Ty Cole/OTTO: 204, 211; © Roger Davies/OTTO: 39, 57, 59, 71, 75, 80, 82, 84, 92, 93, 100, 194; Adrian Dirand: 27; Mark Durling: 63; Tom Fallon: 61; Andrea Ferrari: 189; Joe Fletcher: 60; © Floto+Warner/OTTO: 26, 30, 40, 154; Albert Font: 37; Don Freeman/Trunk Archive: 188; Douglas Friedman: 119; Douglas Friedman/Trunk Archive: 21, 25, 38, 44, 67, 69, 105, 120, 151, 152, 156, 175, 180, 181, 184, 185, 187, 193, 196, 198, 213; Photography by Felix Forest, courtesy of Richards Stanisich: 109; Alfredo Gildemeister: 70; Tobias Harvey: 212; Laure Joliet Photography: 86; Dean Kaufman/Trunk Archive: 23, 107; © Stephen Kent Johnson/OTTO: 98, 116, 132, 133, 160, 166, 177, 200, 205; © Max Kim-Bee/OTTO: 31, 42, 113; © Nikolas Koenig/OTTO: 16, 18, 19, 76; Photography by Peter Krasilnikoff, courtesy of David Thulstrup: 115; Francesco Lagnese: 108, 134; © Francesco Lagnese/OTTO: 141, 165; Massimo Listri: 209; Thomas Loof/Trunk Archive: 34, 53, 66, 94, 117, 136, 143, 169; Spencer Lowell/Trunk Archive: 65; Mark Luscombe-Whyte/The Interior Archive: 56; Magnus Marding/Trunk Archive: 195, 201, 210; JC de Marcos @jcdemarcos: 106; © Michael Moran: 41; © Martin Morrell/OTTO: 28, 171; Nobuaki Nakagawa: 190; Photography by Helen Norman: 140; © Frank Oudeman/OTTO: 202, 215; Skye Parrott/Trunk Archive: 178; Photography by Paolo Petrignani, courtesy of Achille Salvagni Atelier: 95; Eric Piasecki: 73; © Eric Piasecki/OTTO: 51, 54, 55, 74, 78, 89, 91, 125, 127, 128, 138, 139, 147, 148, 149, 158, 161, 172, 173, 176, 192, 208; Rebecca Reid: 123; Coliena Rentmeester/Trunk Archive: 49; © Lisa Romerein/OTTO: 48, 87; Stefano Scata/The Interior Archive: 101, 155; Annie Schlechter/The Interior Archive: 77; Joe Schmelzer/Trunk Archive: 126; Jason Schmidt/Trunk Archive: 68, 142, 150, 168; Fritz von der Schulenberg: 121, 146; © Michael Sinclair: 179; Delfino Sisto Legnani and Marco Cappelletti: 170; Photography by Anson Smart, courtesy of Tamsin Johnson: 135; Photography by Anson Smart, courtesy of Greg Natale: 96, 97, 203, 207; Monica Steffensen: 197; Derek Swalwell: 99, 164; Martyn Thompson/Trunk Archive: 206; © Trevor Tondro/OTTO: 24, 110, 118, 124, 159, 162, 167; © David Tsay/OTTO: 145; Simon Upton/The Interior Archive: 72, 83, 90, 102, 104, 122, 153, 182; Frederik Vercruysse: 64; Wallo Villacorta: 33; © William Waldron/OTTO: 32, 35, 50, 85, 114, 129, 130, 144, 186, 199; © Björn Wallander/OTTO: 17, 43, 45, 46, 47, 58, 79, 81, 88, 131, 137, 157, 163, 174, 183; Joachim Wichmann: 111; Andrew Wood/The Interior Archive: 191.

BIOGRAPHIES

INDIA MAHDAVI

Architect, designer, and scenographer, India Mahdavi is based in Paris. Her studio, created in 2000, is known for the diversity of its international projects that explore the fields of architecture, interior design, scenography, and furniture and object design—all based in one single street in Paris, rue Las Cases. India Mahdavi is known for creating unique environments, combining a modern sense of comfort and elegance with color and humor—a cross-cultural **art de vivre**. Polyglot and polychrome, India Mahdavi has become a signature, offering a special vocabulary that is joyful, cosmopolitan, and elegant all at the same time.

STELLA PAUL

Educated at Harvard University and the University of Southern California, Stella Paul currently lives in New York. At The Metropolitan Museum of Art for twenty-four years, Paul brought audiences and art together, fostering engagement, knowledge, and interpretation for visitors from scholars to students. She served as Museum Educator-in-Charge of Exhibitions and Communication, designing programs, lecturing, teaching, and writing. Before joining the Met, Paul ran Southern California efforts for the Smithsonian's Archives of American Art, a distinguished repository of documentary material and oral history resources.

With museum responsibilities across the widest sweep of chronology and culture, Paul explored connections revealed through broad interdisciplinary study—always with abiding attention to color. In recent years she's written about color in art, architecture, design, and other areas in which color fuels our thoughts and dreams. Her book, *Chromaphilia: The Story of Color in Art*, tracks colors' dazzling mysteries through case studies about materials and meaning spanning millennia. Paul's "I See a Red Door and I Want It Painted Black," introduces *Black: Architecture in Monochrome*. "Seeing Red, Everywhere" was released in *Red: Architecture in Monochrome*, and "Mapping the Colors of the Moon" is published in *The Color of the Moon: Lunar Painting in American Art*.

Phaidon Press Limited
2 Cooperage Yard
London E15 2QR

Phaidon Press Inc.
111 Broadway
New York, NY 10006

Phaidon SARL
55, rue Traversière
75012 Paris

phaidon.com

First published 2021
Reprinted in this compact format 2026
© 2021 Phaidon Press Limited

ISBN 978 1 83729 144 1 American English Edition
ISBN 978 1 83729 196 0 UK English Edition

A CIP catalogue record for this book is available from the British Library and the Library of Congress.

All rights reserved. No part of this publication may be reproduced, stored in a retrieval system or transmitted, in any form or by any means, electronic, mechanical, photocopying, recording or otherwise, without the written permission of Phaidon Press Limited.

Commissioning Editor: Virginia McLeod
Production Controller: Sarah Kramer
Design: Hyperkit
Typesetting: Cantina

Printed in China